# POEMS BY PAMELA

# POEMS BY PAMELA

# POEMS BY PAMELA

For God so loved the world, that he gave his only begotten Son, that whosoever believeth in him should not perish, but have everlasting life. (John 3:16)

## POEMS BY PAMELA

© 2017 Pamela Kay Capages

All rights reserved. No part of this book may be reproduced or utilized in any form or by any means, electronic or mechanical, including photocopying, recording or by any information storage retrieval system without permission in writing from the publisher, except for a reviewer who may quote brief passages in a review to be printed in a newspaper, magazine or electronic publication.

**American Freedom Publications LLC**

www.americanfreedompublications.com

2638 E. Wildwood Road

Springfield, Missouri 65804

ISBN 978-1-64204-647-2 Paperback Version

**Cover Design**  The Kancamagus by Pamela Kay Capages

**Manuscript Editor**  Martin Capages, Jr. PhD

First Edition December 25, 2017

Printed in the United States of America

## POEMS BY PAMELA

## DEDICATION

This book is dedicated to my Lord and Savior, Jesus Christ. God has given me a Joy in my heart because He gave me Jesus who satisfies my soul.

Pamela Kay Capages

**POEMS BY PAMELA**

# ACKNOWLEDGEMENTS

I would like to thank the following people for helping me with my book:

> My husband, Martin for his love and prayerful support in producing this book of poetry.
>
> My dear friend Sheila Young for writing the Foreword to my book and for the encouragement of her mother, the late Helen Scott.
>
> My Serendipity ladies and my friends at the Christian Women's Connection for their positive influence on my life.

# POEMS BY PAMELA

## FOREWORD

Pamela Capages has been one of my best friends since high school. She told me that once, in the middle of the night a few years ago, she was awakened and started writing these amazing poems. She felt they were God-sent. The poems were just spilling out of her. She hadn't written any poetry before, but enjoyed reading poetry. And now, she couldn't stop writing.

My mother recently passed away. When I was unable to be at the hospital, Pamela sat with her the day before she died. She brought Mother her special oatmeal raisin-crisp cookies which are described in one of the poems in this book. You will never eat a better cookie.

She was also there for me after I had breast cancer. She's always doing for others expecting nothing in return. We can talk for hours about anything and everything. She is a devout Christian and active in her church.

If you read these poems you will feel uplifted and see that Pamela's faith is what gives her life meaning. She always says, "Let go and let God be in control". That is why having her as my friend makes me a better person. Just knowing her is a blessing and I thank God for giving me a friend like Pamela.


Sheila Young
Springfield, Missouri

# POEMS BY PAMELA

# POEMS BY PAMELA

## Table of Contents

DEDICATION ................................................................... v
ACKNOWLEDGEMENTS ................................................ vi
FOREWORD .................................................................... vii
PREFACE ......................................................................... xii
POEMS BY PAMELA ....................................................... 1
   Poetry ............................................................................ 1
   Springtime ..................................................................... 2
   Dogwood Delight .......................................................... 4
   Sunlit Wildwood ........................................................... 5
   A Spring Day's Walk With Him ................................... 6
   South Carolina .............................................................. 7
   The Lake Cabin ............................................................. 8
   Queen Anne's Lace ...................................................... 10
   A Mountain View ........................................................ 12
   An Open Door .............................................................. 13
   Sunday Rain Clouds ..................................................... 14
   Summertime Memories ................................................ 16
   Dragonflies ................................................................... 19
   Autumn ......................................................................... 20
   Water's Edge ................................................................ 21
   The Kancamagus .......................................................... 23
   The Ozark Hills ............................................................ 24

# POEMS BY PAMELA

Thanksgiving ................................................................. 25
What Could Be More Satisfying ................................... 27
Beautiful Snow Flurries ................................................. 29
Bethlehem's Babe .......................................................... 30
Tears of Joy ..................................................................... 32
Wintry Night ................................................................. 34
Jesus ................................................................................ 35
My Favorite Things at Christmas ................................. 37
My Christmas Prayer ..................................................... 38
Night Time Noise ......................................................... 39
Oh! Christmas Dear ...................................................... 40
Glorious Sounds at Christmas ..................................... 41
Winter ............................................................................. 43
The Star of Bethlehem .................................................. 45
Look Only To Jesus! ..................................................... 46
Winter Time Blues ........................................................ 48
God Gave Us His children ........................................... 49
Happy Dad's Day ........................................................... 50
Friends ............................................................................ 51
Oatmeal Cookies ........................................................... 52
Grandson Keyser ........................................................... 54
Happy Birthday to Who??? .......................................... 56
Grandson Bailey ............................................................ 57

x

# POEMS BY PAMELA

Granddaughter Jordan ................................................................. 59
Grandson Morgan ....................................................................... 60
Auntie Evelyn's 99th Birthday ..................................................... 61
Two Girlie Girls ............................................................................ 62
Life ................................................................................................ 63
Comparisons ................................................................................ 65
February Landscapes ................................................................... 66
In the Troubled Chaotic Times .................................................. 68
Turn To Thee ............................................................................... 69
Never Alone ................................................................................. 70
If We Believe ................................................................................ 71
ABOUT THE AUTHOR ............................................................ 72

# POEMS BY PAMELA

## PREFACE

MY POEMS

My poems are derived from nature and travel, as well as holiday festive Godly reflections. They are an inherent etching of the fabric of who I am. I always try to give God the glory, honor and praise, because He is my Lord and Savior. Each poem has a subtle, but stirring portrayal of who He is in my life. He is my sole (and soul) purpose for writing poetry!

MY ASPIRATIONS FOR WRITING

My aspirations for writing became very real in the year 2010 as I fervently prayed for God to lead me on the right path as to what He wanted me to do. I have been involved with various acts of creativity all my life. More recently with the Gideon ministry designing and decorating for our conventions and creative writing including some storytelling for another two or three organizations in which I am currently involved. Yet, I had this inner-longing to do something more to serve God. And, I was praying for it to be in an area of writing. I enjoy writing with words that rhyme. My husband encouraged me to consider writing children's books.

# POEMS BY PAMELA

Through the years God had answered prayers and given me so much to be thankful for and I was seeking to serve and love Him in a greater capacity. After many a sleepless night praying for clarity, it was like an epiphany--the answers started flowing in a rather unexpected way.

It was in November 2010 and I was on my way to CWC to hear a Christian author Linda Apple from Fayetteville, Arkansas. As she began speaking from a "Writer's Point of View", Linda talked about the right brain being poetic and the left brain being analytical. I was surprised, because I hadn't had a clue as to the subject of her talk. For just a few minutes, she brought to light the fictional character Bambi to make a point about the era of time in which the book was written. But, what later jumped out at me in the Bambi book was that the author Felix Salten was a poet. He felt nature deeply and he loved animals. When Linda mentioned the name Bambi, I knew that God was clearly telling me that I was to start writing poetry. Only two days before the meeting, I asked for a clear sign or revelation. I had said if the speaker mentions the name Bambi then I would know it was from the Lord. It was a euphoric moment. I was smiling, happy and very excited. My heart was racing just knowing that God had answered my prayer.

# POEMS BY PAMELA

On December 6, 2010, I was propped up in bed with a pad of paper jotting down poetic thoughts that were quickly pouring out. My Christmas poem titled "JESUS" along with "My Christmas Prayer". Suddenly, in the wee hours, my loving husband asked, "What are you doing?" And voila, I wrote enough poems through Christmas for both my children and husband, with a total of six poems for the Christmas season. I then created a covering for the poems to give as gifts. It was the beginning of a wonderfully hidden passion, one that God continues to bless. I told my grandkids--no matter how old you may be, God is never done with you. He gives us each a challenge to serve and glorify Him.

As I mentioned earlier, most of my poems are derived from nature, seasons, holidays, friends and travels. A delightfully funny and somewhat humorous (and true) one written from my childhood is titled "Summertime Memories". The journey has been an amazing experience. I give God the honor, glory, and praise because He has given me the words to express the magnificence of His glory and what He means to me.

Pamela Kay Capages

# POEMS BY PAMELA

## POETRY

Poetry is like a picturesque piece of art
Filling up blank space beginning from the start
Colorfully canvassing a picture to convey
Rhythmically spoken words in a mystic sort of way.

# POEMS BY PAMELA

## SPRINGTIME

My favorite time of the year
Brilliant red dianthus creeping, ah so near
Neighborhood sidewalks on a clear
Afternoon walk with Pup Toby in the rear.

Mom and dad meandering a roadside walk
Breathless to see a few drifting rocks
Shadowy dense tree trunk that appear to block
Sunlight casting images above our mud splattered socks.

Crisp cool air traveling up hill and dale
Over the garden space to every fragrant smell
We notice a grungy brown tail
A red fox lingering beside an open trail.

Oh, for Springtime breezes we inhale
Into the night a slumber deep gale
Bedtime stories fill a memory tale
A pleasant goodnight for one humble male
Dreams that last forever into the summer's evening sail.

# POEMS BY PAMELA

Spring is my favorite time of year
Each new birth brings yet another tawny deer
God's wondrous creations bursting forth seems so surreal
Yet we know with His infinite perfection
He defines life a mystery that is awesomely real!

## POEMS BY PAMELA

## DOGWOOD DELIGHT

As I lay beneath shade of a dogwood tree

Delicate pink buds springing forth so free

I sense God's loving nurturing hand to feed

Each unique tiny blossoming seed

Even the robins are heard singing their song

Tis a vibrant spring day all sparkly calm

Only the flag gently swaying breezes here and gone

March winds ever so light

Bring April showers delight

Man's best friend laying close

Under the tree smelling what grows

Special day in the sun with Mom

While Dad is out fertilizing the yard

Spraying the grass to seasonally guard

Parasites that may attack the beautiful tree

Willfully nurturing our grown sapling for Thee!

## POEMS BY PAMELA

## SUNLIT WILDWOOD

Sunlit wildwood oak trees silhouette shadows below

As Mother Nature's warming clears away the wintry snow

An afternoon stroll down the road in the cold

Green tipped willows sway above the shadowy fold

Squirrels running zigzags while the fox leaves his bed

Springtime is the reason the flower lifts its head

Onto the grassy green lawn that send an awesome spread

God's picturesque backdrops, green, yellow and red.

# POEMS BY PAMELA

## A SPRING DAY'S WALK WITH HIM

With fresh April showers and colorful Spring flowers

Periwinkle blue skies--mine eyes somehow devour

Slumbering overcast clouds lifting their silvery brows

Glimpses of sunlight trickling through just now.


I hear wrestling tree top birds bellowing a high pitch sound

Springtime memories drifting homeward bound

Blue Jay singing his melodic mocking song

God's majestic small voice raising someone's spirit on

A glorious day for observing is ours

Our divine Creator summons rain, sun and moonlit stars.


He orchestrated each twist and turn

Just to bring us more joy than we may grasp to learn

How precious is His way?

When He gave His Risen Son that Easter Morning Day.

# POEMS BY PAMELA

## SOUTH CAROLINA

Ocean Sky--Somber Sweet
Horizon--slate, green, golden wheat
Black--Oceanic white caps meet
O'er the coastline burrowing deep.

Tiny pebbles and seagulls stream
Quite a miraculous joyful scene
Given the day to roam and soar
Against the billowy seaside shore.

People meandering down the wharf
Capturing pictures in the rough
Touches of sunlight filtering through
Palmetto treetops waving hands too.

'Hello' to the folks on Myrtle Beach
For some--they'll come here only to reach
A star-lit night--an ocean view sight
For many good memories--a pleasant good-night!

## POEMS BY PAMELA

## THE LAKE CABIN

A restful retreat amidst the everyday grind
On the deck with a cold glass in hand to unwind
A journey not far from the city to me
Is what makes the weekday a rare vision--you'll see!

A door yet unopened, a surprise fun delight
Then a feeling insurmountable knocks me down at the sight
A zillion brown-spiders, lady bugs and wasp
Sends my head to spinning--one mouth lingering gasp.

A wrangling session that begins with the hose
To water, spray, clean till the clock slows my woes
You're grungy and smelly, time for a shower
Tomorrow will begin in just a few hours.

The humdrum of work never seems to disappear
Nor the dazzling association I feel drawing near
A placid breezy shore line setting below
Breathing in pleasant lake air ever so slow.

I traipse down the hill toward the dock, what a deal
Ah with such ease just to throw in a reel
A few fish respond to the worm on my hook
As if to say they feared I was undoubtedly shook.

# POEMS BY PAMELA

Watching the green ripples wash to the shore
A sudden tranquility fills my heart up to soar
The body relaxes, my mind suddenly free
All the worries and troubles that once seemed to be.

From the hubbub cabin that brought me to Thee
The abundance of gifts so lovingly I see
In life's work and God's world natural beauty
You bring a sense of well-being to all and for me!

**POEMS BY PAMELA**

## QUEEN ANNE'S LACE
[GOD'S AMAZING GRACE]

A lacy wildflower clothed in pure adornment

Does not compare with the perfection of King Jesus' radiant face

Fully vibrant Walnut tree branches

Jesus' uplifted arms give us power and strength

Abidingly present to keep us strong

Bridling our Father's loving Will

He brings comfort in calming us still

Jesus to His Church the Bridegroom calls

In Heaven we'll stand in amazement and awe

Transposed by God's shimmering light

Transformed in God's magnificent sight

Praise God from whom all blessings flow

Our love for Him forever will grow

Thank You Jesus for saving my soul

And thank You Lord for showing your Face

In the beautiful flower of Queen Anne's Lace

JESUS the Sweet Honeysuckle of Amazing Love!

## A COLD SKY

A cold sky--somber gray
Flashes of bright light
Brilliant clouds rumble
A stormy rain covered day.

God's powerful wave
Electrifying the Heavens
The far-off mumbles
Of His mighty rave.

Distance lessening the blow
Of the noisy thunder
Yet still--another boom
Reeks subtle havoc below.

**POEMS BY PAMELA**

## A MOUNTAIN VIEW

A fallen mountainous rocky pitch
Lay o'er the brawny soil so rich
A fertile land--the humus sand,
Yet, can a farmer's plant withstand?

The humid mossy wet terrain
Fuzzy rotten clay remains
Amidst the dampen ground below
The slippery moist, sponge-like hole!

### POEMS BY PAMELA

## AN OPEN DOOR

Over beyond the ocean steep
Lay a treasure swarming deep
Stunning Great White taking flight
Flying around like a skyward kite.

Many a turn and curve they'll take
Raking up scores of fish what make
Bountiful feast for fishermen
Lucky to catch their noonday din.

Like scavengers of great domain
We too find narrowing slim remains
Mother Nature's futile tyranny
Ever present struggle--the irony.

One day in all God's Eternal Glory
Will banish the sea's mystical story
For riches of the ocean floor
Will then expose an open door.

To lavish and dine
No labor of time
An overwhelming presence
The mightiest testy essence.

Equality shared by yet all creatures
To roam the earth--a marvelous feature!

## POEMS BY PAMELA

## SUNDAY RAIN CLOUDS

Sunday rain clouds
Reap rumbles of thunder
Love so amazing
Love so divine.

God's almighty hand
Reaching down from above
Refurbishing Mother Nature
With wet torrents of love.

Stormy wind shadows
Tall Oaks' out-stretched arms
Dispersing dark images
Cascading o'er farms.

A soggy misty canvas
Far-sighted away
A horse drawn carriage
Still mutedly gray.

The distant horizon
Obstructed by haze
An overcast sky leaves only few rays
Of hope for sunlight--albeit for today.

# POEMS BY PAMELA

Ah, surely tomorrow's green sod
Will bring comfort and play
Love so amazing
Love so divine.

POEMS BY PAMELA

## SUMMERTIME MEMORIES

I loved those childhood sun-filled days
The memories all roll into one
A Summertime of outdoor play
My perfect fantasy for backyard fun!

Pouring water into the ready-made sandbox
Daddy had tediously built the frame
Was a labor of love to my Papa Wilcox
An awesome shovel and bucket for me all the same!

A fairytale castle came into its own
My tiny hands spent many an afternoon
Content and happy licking an ice cream cone
Then I'd fill Mother's wash tub to the top and croon!

A sigh of relief for a shriveled-up body
You'd see me plop in and out
Sipping Kool aid, lazy day groggy
A tea party's delight nothing to pout!

Nary a worry, not even a dread
Only once had I tumbled hitting the ground
On my tummy-thank goodness not my head
The homemade swing flipping me upside down!

# POEMS BY PAMELA

A mere few stitches beneath my chin
Very certain to fly, up, up and away
The soft breezes ever so gently send
Me flying over the moon and back for a day!

I wouldn't undo that youngster crazed days
So funny a memory, I retrace
A watermelon seed stuck in my nose, to raise
Surprised looks on Mom and Dad's face!

Back inside my folks were laughing
Cause old Mr. Possum got me to jumping
With him low in the garbage pail hiding
Munching leftovers from our last night's dining!

It wasn't long till sunny days were waning
Dressing up, make believe and favorite stories
Became a thing of yesterday's dawning
Autumn's leaf raking found its glory!

Sis covering her kid sister in fallen leaves
Neighbor's front yard was the gathering place
Under the large maple tree, that I believe
Brought many a smile to a girl saved by Grace!

Those are a few precious memories now
Bathing suits 'round the water hose sprinkler
Catching grasshoppers to scare big Sis...wow!
Then I'd see her jump up and scream, what a stinker!

# POEMS BY PAMELA

My Heavenly Father reminds me how fast the years rolled by
To make a world difference for this grandmother and wife
Yet, I still reminisce with excitement and pride, oh my!
How much those summertime memories have brought such joy to my life!

# POEMS BY PAMELA

## DRAGONFLIES

Colorfully bodied dragonflies,
God's amazing fragile creatures.
Transparently etched wings display,
His beautifully designed features.

They are dainty in appearance, yet,
May be deadly to their prey.
One shouldn't be too quick to overlook or pardon,
The vying beastly eyes they target.
The insect may remove the heads of innocent victims,
And with their mouth eradicate your sunny backyard garden.

Every flower loving butterfly may be sucked in
From dear life to a rapid sudden ending!
The dragonfly's anonymous visit may not be your earthly death
But for the monarch, it may be an untimely last breath.
Another one of God's divinely appointed creatures.
We too face our demise, sooner or later,
That's why we need be ready to meet our Lord and Savior!

## POEMS BY PAMELA

# AUTUMN

God's beautiful leaves of Autumn unfold
Dazzling red, plum, green and gold
Majestic arms bending down
His heavenly hand touching the ground.

Crisp air lending a fragrant smell
Walking outdoors just to sit for a spell
Sniffing a mum or a blue coral bell
Adventure rambling atop Autumn's trail.

Autumn trees a swaying in the breeze
They seem to flutter with such great ease
Sending down tiny seeds to the ground
Germinating tender shoots all around.

Cornstalks and smiley pumpkins one swell reason
We love to celebrate the Autumn season
With hot apple cider and a sugar spiced donut
No sweeter flavor delights an old mother poet!

So, open your doors, meet your neighbors with s'mores
Sending a loving postcard to distant shores
Autumn's picturesque message sent from the heart
Welcoming others to a fresh morning start!

## POEMS BY PAMELA

# WATER'S EDGE

Amidst the day's blue Autumn sky
With driftwood mounted up so high
A hiding place-the tall grassy shore
Black speckled geese that I adore!

Pup Toby and Mom taking a break
Along the banks of Table Rock Lake
The water's edge reflecting the trees
It is really quite something to see!

Shadowy treetop branches wave
O'er the well-hidden cave-below
Fish soaring out of the deep
As if they were dreaming, still half asleep!

A peaceful walk on this sunny day
Oh, my how I'd like to stay
For only a day or two longer
Meandering the trail, I feel so much stronger!

The serenity of God's still waters
Reminds me that He is the potter
Someday in heaven we will thank Him
Singing hallelujah praise Amen!

# POEMS BY PAMELA

For it is to God that we give
Glory, honor, praise to Him
Our most loving Shepherd Lamb
Hallelujah to the Great I Am!

Thank You Jesus for all that You did
To make us sinners brand new again!

POEMS BY PAMELA

## THE KANCAMAGUS

A Fall trip to New Hampshire in October 2010
My husband and I traveled to visit friends and loving kin
Capturing the wonders of New England's sights
Meandering the mountainous moonshine nights
Was something special to embrace
The majestic White Mountain's stony gray face.

Strolling the hills above shimmering waterbeds
Natural wonders quickly turning our heads
Autumn's colors of the season
God's gentle brush strokes are still the reason
To view the forest glades' greenish-golden scape
Tis perfect place to unwind; a quiet peaceful escape.

There it was, the Kancamagus, a beautiful babbling brook
Folks drove from miles around to view the gorgeous scenic look
Every little hidden cranny that borders that cascade
Reflects the Glory of Creation that the Lord had made.

How invigorating was the journey, a bright spot to ponder
God's earthly reflections were calling us up yonder.
The picturesque Kancamagus brings a contented joyful heart
A prayerful early morning is a wonderful way to start!

## THE OZARK HILLS

The Ozark hills still play a monumental part
So many fond memories woven deep within my heart
A superbly rooted heritage beginning from the start
The place I'll always cherish till the day that I depart.

To my Heavenly peaceful home; elaborate and divine
Where the Prince of Peace lives; a secure place, sublime
The Ozark neighboring hills faintly ringing a memorial chime
My final triumphal homecoming with Jesus, Alive!

## POEMS BY PAMELA

# THANKSGIVING

Thanksgiving is a time for giving
Sharing hope with those in need
Blessed assurance in fruitful living
To help the less fortunate, ah indeed.

Godly assistance, tenderly given
Rendering mankind with love and mercy
Heart and soul powerfully driven
Reaching the lost in places like Jersey.

By ultimate strife we press onward
Spiritually heralded to march forward
to finish the race
enjoying God's Grace
A Happy Thanksgiving!

Thanksgiving is the season to be grateful
For doing all one should do to make a difference!
Thanksgiving Day is a time of reflecting
The many things we feel most grateful
For Family, friends, love of home
Gorgeous places together we roam.

# POEMS BY PAMELA

Beautiful skies, ocean water views
Spectacular landscapes, red-purple hues
These are God's creations--we give praise to Him!
For there's nothing grander than recognizing again.

The things oft taken for granted
Freedom of speech to sing my song
Faith and religion are what make my day!
Our grand old flag the USA
For all that it stands--hip-hip hooray!

Thank You God for sending your Son
It is He that we're truly most grateful
for Blessings galore--sent from above
To continually radiate His perfect love.

We praise and adore You, Father, Son, Holy Spirit
What more could we ask this Thanksgiving Day?
Nothing more than being in the presence
of our living Lord and mighty Savior!

I feel totally blest to be called His child
Happy Thanksgiving to one and all!

POEMS BY PAMELA

# WHAT COULD BE MORE SATISFYING

What could be more satisfying
Then sitting near a crackling fire?
Drinking hot scripture tea. . .
Listening to the old mantle clock
Tick --- Tock --- Tick

Wintry blues?
Huh-uh—No!
The skies are blue
Sunshine breaking thru
This cold Sunday afternoon.

Hubby reading "Decision Points"
Defining Times in which we live!
Still yet, another blessed day
To be thankful for health, wealth
And spiritual humanity.

The world forever dawning change
It'll never again be quite the same
God's terra cotta source we seek
A contemplative place to dream
For one day all the world to be
A perfect union--gloriously free
His steadfast love for humanity!

# POEMS BY PAMELA

No more crying, no more pain
Only blissful things we'll see
The ever present earthly conflicts
Moral decay and brief afflictions
Cease to rule man's heart and mind
Insures a loving peaceful rest
Will then abide for all of time.

The fireside flame still slowly kindles
The truth of faith, hope and love
To those whose heart burns for the Kingdom
An inner glow to finally know
The glory of their Heavenly Home!

# POEMS BY PAMELA

## BEAUTIFUL SNOW FLURRIES

Beautiful Snow flurries
Tumbling down
People scurry
Round in town!

Load the kids
School is out
Buy more tidbits
Not to pout!

Ready the sleds
Time for fun
Put on the Keds
A morning run!

Winter myriads of game
A lot of skill
With far less fame
Icy days 'til all is nil!

Mother Nature's frigid weather
Winter snow flurries still to gather!

POEMS BY PAMELA

## BETHLEHEM'S BABE

We heard the singing in Bethlehem
Their awesome voices still proclaim
The birth of Jesus Christ
The King! The everlasting Name!

The day on high
The angels sang
Yule-tide praises
For the Savior's reign!

His birth to honor
God in everything
A Heavenly scene
That Christmas Eve!

The Wise Men brought
Frankincense, myrrh and gold
Their treasures too, would manifold
The everlasting story told.

Whispers of heavenly joy
Were heard o'er the shepherd's flock
For the wondrous message
Of the Bethlehem Boy!

# POEMS BY PAMELA

A new born King
The Prince of Peace
Our Jesus Lord
We Sing!

Happy Birthday, Jesus!

# POEMS BY PAMELA

## TEARS OF JOY

Worthy is the Lamb
Who is--who was
Forever to come.

To redeem His flock
For those who have believed
In the 'Great I Am'.

The true Son of God,
Holy is the King of Kings!
Almighty Savior, God our Lord.

Blessed are they who mourn
For they 'shall' be comforted
At last to be with Thee.

Is to abide in paradise with Him
For all Eternity!

## GOD'S MOST HOLY LAMB

God's most Holy Lamb 'Jesus'
A sacrifice for all the same
To call upon His blessed name
The beloved Savior's only aim.

For His eternal offering
Defeating sinful human greed
Like Adam and Eve--early night
In the Garden--forbidden bite.

Sending a message of self-deception
Rendering God's merciful reception
A choice of inward heart provision
Man's rightful mind decision.

To consecrate his will to Him
God's most precious Holy Lamb
Forever to Him, shall we stand, Faithful!

## WINTRY NIGHT

In the stillness of the wintry night
January blizzard--cold frost bite
Mother Nature's reprieve to sleep
Within the narrow cliffs--so deep.

A lofty breeze--God's own retreat
Where Scarlet feathered friends will meet
Refurbishing their airy nests
Last stormy blast to hasten less.

Still yet, another flight to roam
God's awesome creatures--welcome home!

## POEMS BY PAMELA

# JESUS

The Star of Bethlehem
Atop the Christmas tree
Could it be radiance I see
Reflecting on me?

I wondered at the mystery
Of unforeseen history
The dauntless untold story
Of His Abiding Glory!

The Magi came bearing gifts
To this infant Son, Jesus
Forsaking ne'er to leave us
He died a life of treason.

His undeserving sacrifice
We often ponder why?
A covering for tranquility
To heed the rest of time.

Let's follow then His example
A life of freedom--'Not'!
The misery and courage
Of God's Only Son, Begot!

# POEMS BY PAMELA

We often relish now
To hear the selfless story
The ever-reminiscent question
Of God's unveiling Glory!

He brought to Earth a Savior
To penetrate the hearts of men
The only one true favor
Is to ask Him, please come in.

## POEMS BY PAMELA

# MY FAVORITE THINGS AT CHRISTMAS

Holly and tinsel strung from the tree

Christmas Eve carols sung merrily for thee

Joyful voices proclaiming Christ's love

Silent Night, Holy Night all is calm

Friends and family laughing and giving

In adoration His glorious gift for receiving

God's Holy Word--the birth of His Son

Oh, Little Town of Bethlehem is a song for everyone

Stars shining bright as was the light on Christmas night

Glory to God and to all mankind

These are the things that bring peace of mind

The happiest Christmas is a place to unwind

In the presence of a loving Heavenly Savior so gentle and kind

I love Thee Lord Jesus, forever You are Mine

## POEMS BY PAMELA

# MY CHRISTMAS PRAYER

The One and Holy Jesus
Our most Heavenly Lord God
You sent to earth on Christmas Morn
A most wondrous gift--a treasure.

To captivate the hearts of men's souls
Forever lasting measure
And will mark the graceful test of time
Until one day in Heaven
We live eternally with Him
Forever endless pleasure!

Amen

## POEMS BY PAMELA

## NIGHT TIME NOISE

Deep in my bed
Not far from my head
I hear clickity-clack
Bellowing whistles from the track.

The distant shadowy train
Heard rumbling in the rain
Deep in the hills
Way over the plain.

A night time troll
Thru black balmy coal
Carrying car tow
Of fuel below.

Under the bridge
Of tree covered fringe
The mighty singe
Makes me cringe!

I then shivered and said:
"Glad to be lying,
Still warm in my bed!"

**POEMS BY PAMELA**

## OH! CHRISTMAS DEAR

Oh! Christmas Dear--My Darling
How wonderful the season!
To commemorate the love of Jesus
He 'came' to be the reason!

To tarry and be merry
Life's earthly journey here
Together--forever
His abiding love, my dear!

An effervescent spirit
Our most Holy inspiration
To honor, love and cherish
A Triumphant acclamation!

God sent His Son into the World
For Us, He gave a Savior
He wanted nothing more than
To win the heart of Favor!

And, so this Christmas Season
Let Us give Him--His desire
Lift high the royal banner
For Jesus--God's Almighty Son!

## POEMS BY PAMELA

# GLORIOUS SOUNDS AT CHRISTMAS

Christmas bells ring-a-ling
Hear the little children sing
Hallelujah to the newborn King
Jubilant voices together we sing.

Violins and loud trombones
Cordial men and women own
Blaring horns buzz around the town
Bleeding out their awesome sound.

Tinsel lit trees lending the way
To Every street corner here we stay
Listening to sleigh bells all array
Atop the horse and buggy--we may.

Sing a song to the King of Kings
Oh, for the JOY that He doth bring
Peace and comfort to Him we cling
Saving Grace is an amazing thing.

Majestically wrapped in soft clothing
Mary and Joseph were there with Him
Abiding in the fields, shepherd men
Proclaiming Him their newborn King!

# POEMS BY PAMELA

Christ is why we celebrate
His goodwill to commemorate
Christmas blessings consummate
Jesus's return--for Him we wait.

So never ever take for granted
The Name who often is regarded
Jesus who for our pardon
Came to Earth to relieve our burden.

For it was He who brought joy
Jesus God incarnate employ
Gave His very life to deploy
Everlasting life to each girl and boy.

All we need do is give our heart
To the One to Whom, He sent to impart
The process of forgiveness He sought
Born of a virgin mother was His start.

So, if your mournful eyes shed a tear
Just look to the Lord to draw you near
Call out to Jesus and He'll appear
For only through Christ do we live minus fear.

Hallelujah to Our Newborn King
Merry Christmas Jesus we sing
To You our loving Savior, My King
Bountiful blessings, to Him we cling!
Forever and Ever...Jesus YOU reign!

**POEMS BY PAMELA**

## WINTER

Frozen tree branches hanging low
From the wintry crystal shaven snow
Bringing to earth a silvery glow
God's majestic handiworks hidden below.

Deep in the forest the deer run about
Scavenging berries to feed on their route
Scurrying squirrels bury acorns in doubt
Ample food will soon come about.

Frigid winds chase the bear to his den
Oh, for a warm hibernating barn wren
To nest in comfort with his dear sweet hen
Mother Nature calls the old crow in.

Great horned owls squawk and hoot
Likely story when the fox jumps to loot
Territorial man on the hunt to shoot
Waddles down the path in his big black boot.

That's when Mom called us in to gather
Close to the fireside room, but we'd rather
Be Outdoors in the cold frigid weather
Wintertime snow brings us together.

# POEMS BY PAMELA

Watching and listening jiggles my mind
Childhood memories forever abide
Bundled in snow suits ever to ride
Down snow-covered hills that chill my hide.

Sledding past the street signs fast
Old Jack Frost biting me at last
Got me to thinking about my past
This winter wonderland has been a blast.

Thank You God for all we're given
To appreciate your perfect time and rhythm
I have had fun being driven
To write this poem has been my heaven!

**POEMS BY PAMELA**

## THE STAR OF BETHLEHEM

The Star shone bright that Christmas Night
As Magi traveled toward the Light
'Twas a magnificent clear sparkling sky
That brought them near to hear His cry.

The sweetest sound they'd ever heard
Almost like a singing song bird
The Shepherd keeping watch by night
Gave a gentle sign to stay alight.

For from that radiant manger bed
A newborn Babe was soon well fed
The scriptures of God's everlasting word
The story of His birth would soon be heard.

He came down to Earth from Heaven above
God Incarnate pure in heart like a dove
So, we could know Him as God's only Son
Our abiding Emmanuel, He is the One.

Who touches the hearts of all mankind?
He gives even the least of these to abide
In His precious word He lives with us still
Forever we know in our hearts He is real.

Jesus! You are our bright and shining Star!

**POEMS BY PAMELA**

## LOOK ONLY TO JESUS!

Christmas gifts have been opened--another season ending
All the world settling down to a much-needed rest
From the hustle and bustle of Christmas days' shopping
We hunker down feeling unduly blest.

For God is waiting to hear from us still
Our first place of interest should be to the Lord
Recognizing the significance of keeping Him real
His pathway is the narrow road.

For it was to Him that we honor Christmas
His gift to give glory and praise
Lest we forget the reason is mindless
To our Lord and Savior for Him we should raise.

A song of thanksgiving to worship His life
A selfless existence we know His to be
He joyfully lived even with strife
The scriptures reveal the truth that we see.

Him forever and always to live in our heart
A transfer of peace He bestows to us all
To Jesus we give glory right from the start
For love and mercy are His gentle call.

To remind us the gift He brought from above
His birth, life and death are why we celebrate Jesus
He rose from the dead so that we might find love
God the Father in Him is so very precious.

# POEMS BY PAMELA

So, look to Jesus even after Christmas is past
And give Him the honor, glory and praise
For without His loving spirit we might even cast
A state of confusion to a world made in haze.

The journey we travel is not far away
From the Glory of Heaven to Him we will gain
A life full of blessings forever to stay
The way He intended together we'll reign!

Away from all evil there will never again be
Destructive allusions to hurtfully bring
Down a man, woman and child...to Him, you will then see
A life filled with purpose to serve our great King!

POEMS BY PAMELA

## WINTER TIME BLUES

Winter time blues
Come mightily due
God's lingering gentle touch
To show just how much.

Like a huge cargo ferry
The heavy load we carry
Reminds us to unwind
And, look to Him for kind

Advice securely written
In His word--totally smitten
To understand the reason
For God's untimely season.

A quiet retreat to share in His ways
Sacred moments to these here days
Many a needed prayer left unsaid
Had we not read the Bible in bed.

A purposeful guide to follow
His perfect plan must we swallow
Like partaking of a healthy meal
What better way to end in His will!

## POEMS BY PAMELA

# GOD GAVE US HIS CHILDREN

God gave us His children
To love and adore
A gift of importance
He earnestly implores.

An exuberance of wealth
So freely He gave
To us Mothers and Fathers
We seek to behave.

To handle with tender
Gentle loving hands
The teaching and blessings
His stronghold demands.

The heart of the Father
Was sent down from above
To touch the lives of
Our children with love.

## POEMS BY PAMELA

## HAPPY DAD'S DAY

Happy Father's Day to You, dearest husband of mine
We reminisce the present and our father's gone bye
Tis a blessing to remember all the ways you Dads sacrifice
To build a better life for your children and wife.

We cherish the dedication and pride You ensure
Working the daily grind to provide a future
A comfortable home, slick car and groceries
A constant reminder of the love and the misery.

So, thank You from the bottom of our hearts dear Dads
For your steadfast love drives me mad, not sad
I'm thankful and grateful that our brave men gave
For me--a daughter, wife and mother
You are my fave!

POEMS BY PAMELA

# FRIENDS

Like flowers in springtime
And fireflies at dusk
Friends illuminate life
With a sweet vibrant musk.

Their gentle persuasion
So caring and kind
Like the Father's own hand
Reaching down so divine.

A perfect reunion
None other as sublime
Than a dear friend
Who comforts time after time.

A knock on the door
Come in for some tea
The pleasure is welcomed
Forever with me!

# POEMS BY PAMELA

## OATMEAL COOKIES

There's just something special about oatmeal raisin cookies
Don't know exactly what it is
The sweet aroma permeating from the oven
The chewy crisp texture makes one yearn for yet another!
Am still deciphering rhyme or reason
Why my dear friend's mom defies the day or the season
Sweet Helen simply smiles each time I come breezing
Through the front door with her favorite oatmeal raisin.
Her modest gentle embrace and the smile upon her face
Her rosy radiant cheeks made my day feel complete!
Precious Helen would tell "there's nothing as delicious"
As savoring the rich chewy flavor, yet
She'd only eat one or two each day to maintain her tiny waist!
We laughed a lot reminiscing
beloved daughter Sheila singing Diana Ross
No matter how late the hour, her mom and dad didn't even stir or toss.
Afternoons found us sharing fondest recollections from our past
The good times sketched in our memories lingering days that last
One day in Heaven we three will laugh and joyfully sing with glee
Praising God our Father
And forever sharing oatmeal raisin cookies!

# POEMS BY PAMELA

Post Script: I sincerely believe that the journey of life begins and ends with a heartfelt conversational day. And one tasty cookie shared with a friend might have been lost in an hour unspoken. To feel and taste is what truly brought us together!

I'm very appreciative of the last few years visiting Helen ... we talked about things that were of importance-day to day stuff and our faith!

A very special lady made an indelible difference ... her story, her heart...the tender love expressed from a dear friend's mother! I will never forget all the good times spent at your home, Helen. Those past and present with my dear friend Sheila. I will forever cherish the memories. I love Sheila as I have loved You, Helen! I thank God for You dear friends. So grateful for your love and for your friendship! I will bake more cookies and write more poems; as was spoken by You dear Helen! Every oatmeal raisin crisp cookie will forever be a cherished memory of all the things that truly matter--all the good times--the kind and thoughtful words, laughter, praying together. Those were the warm cozy touches that wove our friendship together. Both here and soon to be there in heaven--our journey home. Our eternal destination bonded together in the Arms of Jesus! Abiding friends forever.

## POEMS BY PAMELA

# GRANDSON KEYSER

A wee but tender lad was I, a small boy albeit three

I think how totally awesome God was holding onto me

How keenly special even then to have me in His loving care!

On my knees right from the start

God lovingly planting seeds within my heart

"Now I lay me down to sleep, I pray the Lord my soul to keep"

As I was falling fast asleep.

Jesus became a beacon of light

There were so many reasons to do what was right

Even when children around me went wrong

I just knew God was in my world to keep me strong.

The lone forgiver of sin

It was for Him

Me-the warrior, I was longing to have been

The Cross of Jesus spoke to me and for all boys and men.

I recall Him saying, "Dear son, Keyser, remember who You are in the Lord Jesus!"

He said, " I am your God the Father, I will love YOU forever" Amen!

# POEMS BY PAMELA

Post Script: I believe in my heart dear Grandson that God has a divine calling that is 'special' just for You. So never forget who You are in Christ Jesus! After we accept Jesus into our heart the Bible says we are new creations in Christ. We are set apart from the world. Live not as the world lives, but always put your love, trust and hope in Him. He will give you strength to do what is right. Stay in His word. Do what the Bible says is rightful living in God's eyes; believing God will use You for His good purpose. He uses student athletes who don't let what others think or say bring them down or try to influence. All the while holding onto faith, staying strong, being obedient to please God; always and foremost being an example as Jesus is our example! You are one of the elect--You can do this dear grandson! I believe in You, Keyser, and even more, God believes in You!

## POEMS BY PAMELA

# HAPPY BIRTHDAY TO WHO???

Why it's Our Girl, Cami Lou!!
Just one more greeting,
We are sending to YOU!

To help C e l e b r a t e
Your Big Number Seven!
Sure 'Not' to be late
To blow 'Out' the candles!

A dazzling smooth bite,
Mother's homemade surprise
With sparkle and glitter
Her cake--sheer delight!

We hope you will know
After reading these words
Just how much we love You
Granddaughter, 'YOU' Go!

Happy Birthday, Cami

## POEMS BY PAMELA

## GRANDSON BAILEY

I remember well those first few days holding You close in my arms
At only three months before Christmas Day
I was overwhelmingly excited to say...
How much I loved those big brown eyes so full of love and charm!

You never stopped smiling
Day after day your smile only grew bigger
As you scarfed up your food with such vigor
Healthy and strong found our boy outdoors playing.

Your world was beginning to take shape
You were tall in stature ready to trek mountains
Asserting yourself skipping over cracks and fountains
A day in the life of Bailey picking up snakes without even the slightest bite or scrape.

You were on your way
To becoming an athlete
Kicking the ball felt so natural, you were ready to compete
Performing well on the soccer field was an invigorating day.

We enjoyed watching you grow up
Never a dull moment to ponder
A fun filled day of interesting experiences leaving us all the fonder
With a heart for animals you lovingly embraced each scruffy rescue pup.

# POEMS BY PAMELA

An intelligent young man now in college
You're all grown up, a studious student
Devoted to studying, forever prudent
Your most ardent endeavor, skillfully striving for knowledge.

You are making the mark of excellency
Staying focused with good study habits isn't at all a quirk
Aggressively striving to reach your goals' work
Pursuing a career in civil engineering, especially!

We are proud of You dear grandson
And look forward to seeing You graduate with honors
Burning the midnight oil shall prove you all the stronger
To becoming the man God designed You to be in His perfect time and season.

I pray for You to know Jesus in your heart as Savior
He is the One who'll make life complete
For all of life's dreams cannot truly meet
Our everyday comings and goings--that's why we need Jesus our Savior!

## POEMS BY PAMELA

# GRANDDAUGHTER JORDAN

You hold a special place in our heart
There was something unique in You right from the start
An innocent quirky smile, a gesturing crinkly pink hand
Gramma and Grandpa think 'You' are wondrously grand.

Softly singing lullabies on a cold winter's holiday
Reading short stories, we fondly replay
Your singing Jack and Jill brings a sunshiny ray
A huge smile, we didn't know just how to say.

How much fun to sing, dine and play
Throwing a basketball or painting our nails "hooray"
For all the fun times spent in one day
We love You so much that we feel some dismay.

To think that you're graduating high school in May
Can this really be happening a few days away?
We know you'll graduate in style and with honor
And the career You select we anxiously ponder.

Stay true to your heart and to your dream
As You head to Mizzou, it may daringly seem
Like a magnitude of things all brand new
Yet, before You blink we'll be applauding then too!

So, we ask God's watchful eye over You each day
The joy and pleasure will forever stay
Deep in our hearts all together we'll pray
The Good Lord keep You in His loving care all of life's way!

# POEMS BY PAMELA

## GRANDSON MORGAN

Morgan, you were our first-born bundle of JOY!
A spunky blue-eyed, blonde baby boy
At only three months, I saw a radiant sparkle in your eyes
The Good Lord had a unique plan for your life.

Your whimsical cute smile brought such joy to our day
Incredibly sweet, quick to mumble and say
"Apple", the food clearly spoken from your highchair
Seeing your wit and smarts made us happily aware.

We'd soon be chasing ducks at Cumberland Park
And sliding down the slide to excitedly mark
Many more events like fishing at Table Rock Lake
The big bass pulling you around, watch out--a snake!

Your gregarious dad and grandpa
Playing catch with a football
The years of fun suddenly flew by
But you were still the same good hearted little guy.

How very quickly you were turning from an active little boy
Now a young man inventing your own games and a big car toy
Like your dad enjoying the great outdoors, hiking on an open trail
While working to be a successful career-minded male.

Recounting all the many wonderful blessings to show
Just how fond our memories continue to grow
We wish you the best in life, grandson Morgan
May God richly bless you with His love in every new season!

## POEMS BY PAMELA

# AUNTIE EVELYN'S 99TH BIRTHDAY

This honorable title is sure to convey
To dainty Mrs. Evelyn who's Queen for A Day
Her kind gentle spirit is wonderfully real
Not a more noble person in short will reveal
Someone who is sweet with unconquerable wit
Not fooled by Stevie Boy-not one little bit
With her raze dazzle sense of good humor
It blows my mind
To think she is now 99!
Yet, we'll all have to agree
We won't be surprised
The minute her 100th birthday
Comes calling---Oh My!

Post Script: My Auntie Evelyn was my dad's sister who passed away just shy of age 102. She was the mother of my fantastic cousins, Mary, Anne, Mark, and Eric in upstate New York. Mary's husband, Steve (and sometimes Anne's husband, John) would kid Auntie Evelyn about almost everything but she never let them get the best of her.

## POEMS BY PAMELA

# TWO GIRLIE GIRLS

Some years ago, two girlie girls met
A divine appointment from God's pure heart
We had a connection right from the start
Purely spiritual blessings together and yet.

Our sweet friendship continued to grow over time
Never once did I see you waver
From numerous gestures of kindness to savor
Made the relationship even more fine.

You came into my life that glorious day
Bringing genuine love and affection
An instantaneous favorable reaction
We honored each with a smiling sunshiny ray.

Post Script: This poem was written to my dear sweet friend Linda McMurry for her birthday! Linda became a special friend after attending a few meetings at Christian Women's Connection. Linda, always stay the beautiful person that you are today!

**POEMS BY PAMELA**

# LIFE

Life isn't easy, life can be hard

Life is but rather a noble obedience

Finding faith is truly by Him.

It is through serving and following

Putting your whole heart to work for Him

Jesus followed the will of His Father

Shouldn't we do the same for Him?

Abidingly seeking His will to do good and what is right

The business at hand is not our pleasure, but His

For He gave His whole body and heart to mend a broken world

He knows what's best for us even from the start

We can never repay Him the debt that is ours

Only believe in the Father to give Jesus your heart

First place in your life is the measure of His Glory

It isn't the fame or the tangible things

# POEMS BY PAMELA

It isn't the same to find pride in oneself

It is through God's love that we find peace and comfort

In a world lost to greed

Only God's love and mercy will suffice

For the real pleasure we seek

Is the heart of the Father

Pouring down His perfect love

That comes through His Precious Son--He is the One!

Who gives both the gift of Grace, salvation and everlasting life!

**POEMS BY PAMELA**

## COMPARISONS

Skeletal tree branches
Human frailty

Exposure to the elements
Emotions riding high

Elevated blood pressure
Rising temperature

Melting snow
Losing hold

Grasping for air
Oxygen nowhere

Audacious laugh
Company's draft

Earth eruptions
Life's interruptions

Brilliant performance
Clear blue skies

## POEMS BY PAMELA

## FEBRUARY LANDSCAPES

A spectacular sight those Mississippi flat pines
There slender needled arms reflectively define
God's majestic rambling ridged green hills
His creation a praiseworthy thrill.


The coastline bay brought much to enjoy
Sunny blue sky, wet craggy soil
Turning away from the strong brutal winds
We discover a quietness that we hope never ends.


The Gulf of Mexico's beautiful bluish green wave
Brings back memories of Palm Harbor I still crave
The rolling sea resurfacing a few coupled dolphins
Delighted our gulf stroll round Clearwater bend.


The fresh salty marsh dune rushes
Nestled among the secluded palmetto branches
Are a lovely attraction for those who will walk
The Grand Lagoon at Saint Andrews State Park.

# POEMS BY PAMELA

Picking up seashells on Panama beach
While listening to the gulf shores echoing screech
White seagulls flying o'er our head
Still swooping down to the sea water again.

The warm sun shone bright that February day
As I felt the rays on my shoulder
they may
Bring a surge of color instead of dismay
As I return home on a cold winter's day.

**POEMS BY PAMELA**

## IN THE TROUBLED CHAOTIC TIMES

In the troubled chaotic times we're living
Conspicuously heavy-laden hearts do tarry
Clearly momentous strife and worry
Everyday struggle--much to carry
An unsettling rest
A world in distress
A dreadful mistrust
Disorderly stress
A near perfect resolution to
The power of chaos and terror
Is to fall upon knees in prayer
To diminish current selfish error
Of left and right tactics
The government's hand--an injustice
Of sabotaging the Nation's free will
To execute their own harmful crisis
An on-going perplexing situation
To combat threat and evil
The world needs Jesus Christ in their hearts
To rid the darkened guise of the devil.

**POEMS BY PAMELA**

# TURN TO THEE

Once we have turned from futility to Thee

We have no further fruitless deed

Our lives then lean toward the One we need

It is He that brings new life for seed

To read the Holy Scripture we will feed

On the Word of Him who died indeed

To remove all guilt and sin we heed

The ultimate price He paid me to lead

Others on the path to free

a lost read

Down the narrow road they too may feed

Bringing eternal life to those in need

Precious time here to share Him indeed

It is all about You Most Holy Lord!

### POEMS BY PAMELA

## NEVER ALONE

Imagine the tiniest gesture

Bringing joy to a mournful heart

A soft word gently spoken

Soothing a dear and hurting soul

A soft hand holding that of another's

Can be such a comforting touch

We never know how sweet the measure

Until we too have journeyed there alone

God in His mercy brings us Angels

His unwavering loving kindness is steadfast

He is teaching His children to be more like Jesus

To run with endurance the road less traveled

A bridge over troubled waters may just be hidden treasure

To remind us each we are never truly alone

God paves the way to those who seek

His guiding light will brighten the way

To find our final peaceful heavenly home

To God the Father and His Son Jesus

The ultimate quest adorned with Him!

**POEMS BY PAMELA**

## IF WE BELIEVE

If we believe and trust God in all that we think, do, and say

He surely will bless and keep us safe and humble on life's journeying way

The narrow path may oft seem hard to transcend the rocky granite peak

Yet drawing from His grace and strength, the course will not seem nearly as bleak.

# POEMS BY PAMELA

## ABOUT THE AUTHOR

**Pamela Kay Capages**

My midwestern upbringing was one of new beginnings after Mom and Dad, Louise and Bill Wilcox, settled in Springfield, Missouri. Upon first arrival to the Show-Me State, my parents were all about setting up home. Both Dad and Mom loved the ideal perfect weather and the scenic rolling hills located close to beautiful lakes. Plus, they thought the Ozark's seasonably warmer climate would be a wonderful place to raise their family. My folks were forever reminding my sister and me of how they walked to school in knee-high-boots amid 3 ft. deep snow drifts in Oneonta, NY. My dad's promotions with J. J. Newberry's and the resulting relocations had begun to wear on my mother. But with the prospect of moving to Missouri, they jumped at the chance for Dad to manage the Springfield J. J. Newberry's store.

A couple of years had passed by and along came "number two" daughter as my dad often referred to me. By then, my older sister had turned six. A few years later, to avoid another job transfer, Mom and Dad opened their very own variety store called A. W. Wilcox 5 & 10. Inside the store my parents had setup a delightful soda, hamburger and chili bar. There were bins chuck-full of the old fashion hard and chewy

# POEMS BY PAMELA

candy. This was a child's perfect paradise to embark upon each new day. Although years later, making frequent visits to the local dentist proved I had eaten far too much candy! A good lesson learned.

I have fond memories of playing at the store with other neighborhood children and in my backyard-a small city girl enjoying the simple things of life. I had fun in junior high where I met Sheila (Scott)Young who would become one of my best friends in high school.

In high school, I was more interested in socializing than studying. One day I was caught talking too much and was sent to the dean's office! This was a study hall class and the boys football coach signaled me to come up to his desk. Seemed like, with his snarky smile, he was picking on me. After that experience, I was never quite as much the social butterfly. Sheila and I finished high school together and went on to attend college at SMS, now Missouri State University. We have stayed in touch as close friends. God is so good to have blessed our friendship with deep roots. It is wonderful the heartfelt love and closeness that we feel. Our husbands are friends and we have children that attended the same schools. We have come full circle.

My husband Martin and I have five children and seven grandchildren between us. We are active in our church and in The Gideon's International and Auxiliary. For many years I have been associated with Christian Women's

# POEMS BY PAMELA

Connection, as well as my Red Hat Women--some of my very special Christian friends. I have also worked with the children's ministry in my Church. There have been many other blessings including 25 years as a member associate with the Springfield Art Museum. But most of all, I am most grateful to my beloved mother and father for rearing me in a Christian home so that I could know Jesus as my Lord and Savior.

Pamela Kay Capages

# POEMS BY PAMELA

# POEMS BY PAMELA

## POEMS BY PAMELA

I can do all things through Christ who strengthens me. (Philippians 4:13)

# POEMS BY PAMELA

www.ingramcontent.com/pod-product-compliance
Lightning Source LLC
LaVergne TN
LVHW041536060526
838200LV00037B/1018